EXCEL VBA

A Step By Step Guide to Learn EXCEL VBA

ELITE TECH ACADEMY

Copyright © 2019 by AmazingLifeForever

All rights reserved.

This document is geared towards providing exact and reliable information in regards to the topic and issue covered. The publication is sold with the idea that the publisher is not required to render accounting, officially permitted, or otherwise, qualified services. If advice is necessary, legal or professional, a practiced individual in the profession should be ordered.

From a Declaration of Principles which was accepted and approved equally by a Committee of the American Bar Association and a Committee of Publishers and Associations.

In no way is it legal to reproduce, duplicate, or transmit any part of this document in either electronic means or in printed format. Recording of this publication is strictly prohibited and any storage of this document is not allowed unless with written permission from the publisher. All rights reserved.

The information provided herein is stated to be truthful and consistent, in that any liability, in terms of inattention or otherwise, by any usage or abuse of any policies, processes, or directions contained within is the solitary and utter responsibility of the recipient reader. Under no circumstances will any legal responsibility or blame be held against the publisher for any reparation, damages, or monetary loss due to the information herein, either directly or indirectly.

Respective authors own all copyrights not held by the publisher.

The information within this book is offered for general informational purposes solely, and is universal as so. The presentation of the information is without contract or any type of guarantee assurance. While we try to keep the information up-to-date and correct, there are no representations or warranties, express or implied, about the completeness, accuracy, reliability, suitability or availability with respect to the information, products, services, or related graphics contained in this book for any purpose.

The trademarks that are used are without any consent, and the publication of the trademark is without permission or backing by the trademark owner. All trademarks and brands within this book are for clarifying purposes only and are owned by the owners themselves, not affiliated with this document.

The author claims no responsibility to any person or entity for any liability, loss or damage caused or alleged to be caused directly or indirectly as a result of the use, application or interpretation of the information presented herein.

Created with Vellum

CONTENTS

Introduction	vii
1. Excel VBA Overview	1
2. How VBA Works with Excel	11
3. Programming Concepts	23
4. Essential VBA Language Elements	31
5. VBA Data Types	35
6. VBA Sub and Function Procedures	57
7. Introducing the Excel Object Model	77
8. Error-Handling Techniques	83
9. Exercises: VBA Programming Examples and Techniques	97
10. Advanced VBA Techniques	123
Conclusion	135
References	137

INTRODUCTION

Excel VBA which is also referred to as Visual Basic for Applications in Excel is a sophisticated and powerful programming language that enables users to write their own commands or functions in Excel. The custom functions help users by easing their tasks and enabling them to execute tasks much faster. With Excel VBA one is capable of accomplishing thousands of tasks with a lot of efficiency.

VBA is the programming language understood by most of the Microsoft Office applications so all the programming required in any of the office programs should be executed in VBA. The Visual Basic for Applications exists within Office applications therefore it can be used as a medium for accessing and also interacting with the object model of the host applications. VBA therefore knows things such as Workbooks, Worksheets, charts and cells.

As much as Microsoft Excel is fully packed with several tools, it still lacks all one needs to perform the daily tasks such as creation of custom functions, automation of tasks and execution of repetitive tasks. VBA comes as a gap filler that enables users to write their own commands and methods that they can use to perform specific tasks. Once you get a good grasp of Excel VBA, you will never get stuck in your work as a result of lacking the built-in tools you can use to execute the tasks.

Excel VBA is a book that has covered in detail all you need to know about this programming language and how you can use it to perform various tasks such as automation, creating custom commands in excel, creation of a set of instructions several times, creation of custom function and custom add-ins in Excel amongst others. Whether you already have some basic understanding of a given programming language or zero experience with programming; this book has been written in a step-by-step way that makes it possible for the reader to grasp all of the necessary information even without any prior knowledge in programming.

Take your time and read the book through to the end for quality insight on how to make use of this versatile feature in Excel. The knowledge you will gain after reading the book will enable you to create applications that are customized for your needs. You will therefore be able to use Microsoft Excel in a more effective and efficient way. It's important to note that the book has been written with beginners in mind so even without any coding background, you can still get the most out of the book. The chapters build on each other, so skimming and skipping through the book may not provide the desired benefit.

So let's get started, shall we?

Chapter One
EXCEL VBA OVERVIEW

*E*xcel VBA has been used by many people to help in saving time and reducing work related headaches. Excel VBA enables users to execute a number of tasks with limited time and effort. Visual Basic was first released in 1991 and was designed to allow for easy construction of Windows programs complete with standardized graphical interfaces that users of the operating systems are familiar with.

Microsoft had distributed versions of the Basic programming language for decades however those were designed for use in command-line environments such as Microsoft's DOS operating system and not for use in the modern graphical operating systems. VBA was designed to be a fully-fledged programming language complete with features such as string processing, computation and more. It was integrated with drag-drop approach that's ideal for building user interfaces making it quite easy to use even by beginners.

WHAT IS VBA?

VBA refers to Visual Basic for Applications. Excel VBA is a programming language that enables creation of user-defined functions and automation of specific computer calculations and processes. Visual Basic Application is a standard feature for Microsoft Office products used for Excel and other Microsoft Office Programs such as PowerPoint and Word. All the Office suite programs share a common programming language. The language can be used for making some sophisticated workbooks or applications that are user defined. This powerful built-in programming language enables users to easily incorporate functions that are user written into a spreadsheet. VBA has been derived from Visual Basic 6 that was the mostly used programming language until the introduction of .NET by Microsoft.

VBA is considered as the core macro language for all of the Office applications and it has been incorporated into the software with the help of other vendors. VBA may not be great for building sophisticated and big applications however it's great at getting tasks done much faster and more easily. It's great at building Excel-based applications and automating Excel. If VBA is to be considered useful then you don't have to write complicated programs. Knowledge of VBA is however critical as it will make it easier to analyze problems that are relatively complex. To effectively use Excel VBA, one should have some basic knowledge of Excel alongside use of the named ranges and built-in functions.

In VBA users get to type commands into an editing module so as to create a macro. Macros enable users to generate customized reports and charts automatically, alongside performance of various data processing functions. Macros help with automating tasks and merging program functions in a way that enables developers to build custom solutions through use of Visual Basic. The Visual Basic applications require a code to run within a host application like Excel since it can't operate as a standalone application. VPA for Excel has been used in the finance industry for creation and maintenance of complex financial spreadsheet models. VBA has also been used to create trading, pricing and risk management models, generation of financial ratios and to forecast sales and earnings.

VBA is quite user intuitive and enables even those with very little or even no computer programming knowledge to easily learn. It is an event-driven programming language that is designed specifically to customize applications that contain the Visual Basic for applications and application programming interface (API). VBA helps in controlling Microsoft Excel functionality and any other Microsoft Office Application.

Before getting into the details of VBA, it's important that one has expectations that are appropriate. If you are into performing many tasks then you should be aware that VBA is quite simple to use. Creation of simple add-in functions in VBA is generally easy. It's also important to know that you can possibly do anything by using VBA. If there is anything you can dream of doing in Excel then know that you will be able to do it with VBA. As much as acquiring information is important; it's also important to know that you will not be able to effectively learn VBA by reading books only as it will be quite complex having to memorize all of the commands.

If you're a serious user of Microsoft Excel then it's important to note that VBA can help you extend the power of Excel in a great way. When working with Excel becomes repetitive, you need a macro so as to automate the tasks and for that to happen you will need VBA. VBA has been removed from the menu overtime and is converted into an option so that beginners may not feel confused or intimidated by it. All of the versions of Excel work in a similar way once you write a program.

WHAT CAN YOU DO WITH VBA?

Excel VBA helps in turning complex or time-consuming tasks into automated processes that in turn help save time and improve work quality and reporting. For example, a sales person could create a button that aids printing of weekly report for the present week before the start of a meeting. The task can be simplified by having a data analyst download data then run a macro to format, delete and rearrange the data right before outputting into a pivot table. All these can be executed with just one macro.

VBA can be used in keeping customers names or any other data, creation of forms and invoices, analysis of scientific data, budgeting and forecasting and development of charts amongst other tasks. Various companies have also used VBA to add programming capabilities to their applications. VBA is also implemented in applications that have been published by other companies such as AutoCAD, CorelDraw and SolidWorks amongst others. VBA enables an application like Excel to internally run a program and provide customized version of Excel for a given purpose.

VBA contains all of the statements and functions that are

necessary for creating robust Windows applications. Some of the tasks that can be performed with VBA include;

- Creation of instances of objects within your code.
- Creation of classes (reusable custom software objects)
- Linking databases such as Access and SQL Server to ODBC.
- Integration with messaging API to create exchange/mail applications.
- Integration with Intranet and Internet solutions.
- Creation of custom dialog forms and boxes.
- Storage and retrieval of data from the windows registry.
- Detecting and handling of errors.
- Incorporation of Active X controls into application interface.
- Passing of data between the VBA enabled applications with minimum programming.
- Passage of data between VBA enabled application from within first VBA-enabled application.
- Control of Office applications; almost 100% of Office products functionality is exposed as objects, methods and properties which therefore mean that whatever you can do with the application's interface you can equally do programmatically except with a few exceptions.
- Automation of any task that can be undertaken from the keyboard, menus or mouse.

ADVANTAGES AND DISADVANTAGES OF VBA

VBA is a simple programming language that is used within Excel to develop macros and other complex programs. The structure of this basic programming language is quite simple, especially in reference to the executable code. VBA is not just a language but also an integrated and interactive development environment. The VB-IDE is highly optimized for the support of rapid application development. It's normally easy to develop graphical user interfaces and be able to connect them to other handler functions that are provided by the application.

Here are some of the advantages of VBA;

Easy to Learn

Visual Basic is never complicated for an average programmer. The syntax is quite straightforward when compared to other programming languages. The Visual Basic environment is considered to be top notch and very easy to understand. There are also a number of online forums that provide tutorials and answers to some of the common problems. The code is also easy to write and database connectivity is also high.

Widespread applicability

VBA is widely used throughout the programming community majorly because it provides an extremely rapid application development (RAD) when compared to other programming languages. As much as the use of VBA is restricted to Microsoft's operating systems; it's still being used widely within the programming community. VBA is appropriate for GUI applications such as databases and front-end. It therefore enables programmers to make programs that are much better than is possible with programming languages such as VC++, Power builder and Delphi.

Automation and repetition

VBA is efficient and effective when handling repetitive solutions to correction of problems or formatting. For example if you have to change the style used in a paragraph at the top of each page in Word or format multiple tables that have been pasted from Excel into a Word document or even make changes into multiple Outlook contacts, then you need to consider automating the tasks with VBA. If it's some change that you need to repeat several times then use of VBA is worth considering. Any formatting or editing that you can do manually can also be done with VBA.

Extensions to User Interaction

There could be times when you intend to encourage users to interact with a document or an Office application in a specific way that's not part of the standard application. VBA can help in extending user interactions.

Interaction between office applications

Whether you intend to copy all of your contacts from Outlook to Word then have them formatted into a specific way, or you intend to move data from Excel to a given set of PowerPoint slides, then you can make use of VBA programming to interact with details of different applications at the same time. You can easily modify content in one application based on content that exists in another application.

Other advantages of Visual Basic for Applications include;

- The graphical user interface of VB-IDE provides users with intuitively appealing views for management of program structure in various types of entities such as modules, classes, procedures and modules.
- VBA provides users with a comprehensive content sensitive and interactive online help system. The structure of VBA is also quite simple since it's not just a programming language but also an integrated interactive development environment.
- VBA is built around the .NET environment that's used by all of Microsoft's visual languages so quite a lot by done in Visual Basic just like in other languages.
- The ability to do the same tasks that are normally done in Excel much faster.
- Ease in working with huge sets of data
- Reporting of programs from large central databases such as SQL Server, financial and production protection programs
- It's easier to find answers to programming problems when using VBA than with other programming languages.
- VBA is more of a component integration language that's attuned to Microsoft Component Object Model (COM) and can be written in diverse languages and then integrated with the Visual Basic.

DISADVANTAGES OF VBA MEMORY CONSTRAINTS

VBA requires a great deal of memory for its initial installation so that it can function efficiently after installation. VBA is a GUI-bases development tool that has graphical aspects and requires a substantial amount of space. Many programmers also argue that C-languages have a declaration of arrays that's much better. Programmers can therefore use C-languages to initialize several structures at declaration time. This is not possible with VBA.

VBA is also not great for making programs that require a lot of processing power and time such as games.

Here are other disadvantages of VBA;

- Majority of the applications developed in Visual Basic only work on Windows Operating Systems and is mostly supports graphics and database applications.
- When compared to C, C tends to have better declaration of arrays which makes it possible to initialize a range of structures in C at declaration time.
- VBA is a powerful programming language however it's much slower when compared to other languages.

Chapter Two
HOW VBA WORKS WITH EXCEL

Microsoft Office applications are designed in a way that exposes things which are referred to as objects and receives instructions in a way that's similar to how a phone works. In VBA users interact with the application by forwarding instructions to numerous objects within the application. Most of the objects are expansive but also have their limits as they can only execute that which they are designed to do, as instructed by the user.

For example; a user can open a document in Word and make changes then save and close it. In VBA programming; Word exposes a document object through use of a VBA code and the user then instructs the document object to execute tasks such as open, save or close. VBA is one of the most complex features in Excel. If you have some background in object-oriented programming language such as Java, C++ or any other, then you can easily grasp the VBA idea. VBA code is normally written in a VBA module so as to perform functions in Excel. VBA modules are normally stored in the Excel workbook and any number of the VBA modules may be stored in a workbook. VBA modules consist of procedures - blocks of computer code used to perform several actions.

A VBA module may have function procedures as well. A function procedure performs calculations internally then returns a single value. A function can also be called from another VBA procedure and also be used as a function in a worksheet formula directly. VBA also works with objects and Excel has over 100 built-in objects. Almost everything one creates is in the object and examples of some objects are whole Excel, a worksheet, a workbook, a cell range on a worksheet, rectangle shape and a chart.

∼

GETTING STARTED WITH THE VISUAL BASIC EDITOR

The visual basic editor is the workplace for creating the VBA code and the editor can be accessed through Developer tab. The shortcut to accessing developer is ALT + F11. The editor will then be displayed in a separate window and each of the programs in the Office suite has its own VBA editor. You can turn the Developer tab on by executing the following steps.

Right click anywhere within the ribbon then select on customize the ribbon.

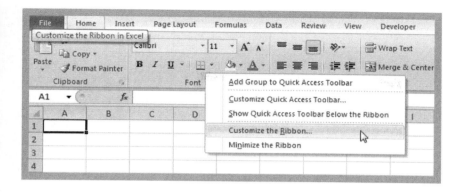

Under customize the ribbon, towards the right side of the dialog box, select main tabs then select the developer check box. Click on OK once done.

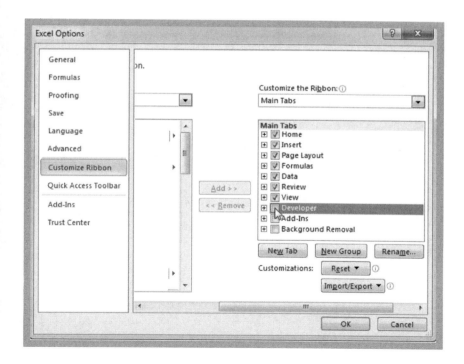

You will then be able to view the developer tab.

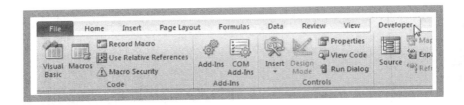

To add a command button on your worksheet, move to Developer tab then click on insert. Select Activex Controls group then click Command Button.

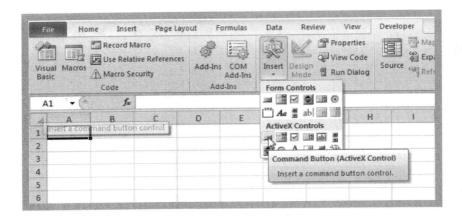

Drag the command button to your worksheet. To assign a macro to the command button; click the command button. Ensure that the design mode is selected then click view code.

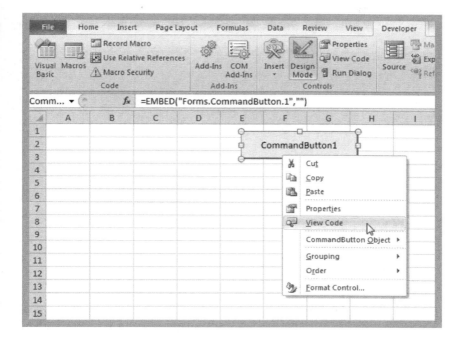

The visual basic editor will then appear. Place the cursor between Private Sub Command Button1_Click () then end sub. You can then add the code line as shown.

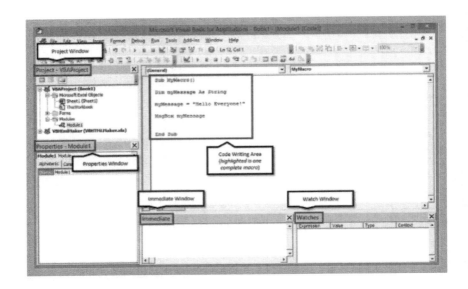

Project Window

This window shows all the files that have been opened and uses a tree view where you can go deeper into each of the open files and see the areas where the VBA code can be inserted. The image above has two files that are open in the Excel application. Book1 has 3 sub folders;

Microsoft objects: This folder hosts a code area for your workbook and your workbook spreadsheets (Sheet1)

Forms: This folder is storing any user forms that you create. In case you don't see this folder then add it by right-clicking at any place within the projects folder tree. You can then go to insert>form.

Modules: A module folder stores macro and the function code. If you don't see this folder it means the project may not have any macro code in it. The code can still be stored in the objects or forms folder. This folder can be added by right clicking any place within the projects folder tree by going to Insert>Module.

Properties Window

The property window enables users to modify certain aspects of object, form or module that have been highlighted. You can give your forms or modules a more meaningful name than the default names provided by the visual basic editor. Custom names within the name field can only be one word in length.

Code writing area

The code writing area is the place to write and edit your VBA code. Each of the macros should begin with a Sub statement and is opened with Sub(insert macro name) ( ) then close with end Sub). The VBA editor color codes some of the keywords in different colors and this helps in making the code look more organized. When learning how to write VBA code, you can consider the following;

Use Indentations: Try to use indentations always through the Tab key within your code. There are a number of methodologies to tabulating code however you need to be consistent as it will help when trying to either add or debug your code. It will also be helpful when another person is trying to help with coding.

Write in Lowercase: Every word in VBA language has at least one capitalized letter. It's important to note that visual basic editor is not case-sensitive and will correct you when necessary. It therefore means that when you type "workbook" the editor will autocorrect and change it to Workbook. You can type everything in lowercase and if in case the basic editor doesn't capitalize at least a letter, you will know you have either misspelled the word or it's not defined.

Having the Visual Basic editor help in correcting every word can really help in making your code less buggy and ease frustration that may arise.

Immediate Window

The immediate window enables users to do all manner of tests while they write and run codes. You can use code Debug.Print to notify VBA to send information that follows into the immediate window. This could either be the output value of a given function, value of a cell, or whatever the current application property is set to. The immediate window is normally hidden by default and a shortcut Ctrl + g can be used to view it. Consider incorporating its functionality into code writing and testing processes.

Watch Window

The watch window shows all of the data that is stored within a variable. Some of the variables, like those you create in your code, may not have much data stored in them. However if you are to view a variable assigned to a cell then you may see data such as value, height, font, color, fill color and more. This is useful especially when trying to debug code and understand the value of your variable at any given point within your code.

If you are to watch a variable then you should highlight your variable text then click on the add button (the eyeglasses icon that's located at the debugging toolbar). You will then be able to see the variable appear at the watch window. Once you begin to run your code through and load a value to the variable; you should see an option a plus sign then drill down or even expand out the contents stored in the variable.

OBJECTS IN EXCEL VBA

Most programming languages deal with objects through a concept referred to as object-oriented programming language. Excel VBA object is more like a tool with certain functions and properties and also contains data. An Excel worksheet is considered an object; the range of cells are also considered as an object or anything with specific functions and properties and contain a data. In order to view the objects, click on the object browser and a list of objects will be presented alongside their properties with the methods as shown below.

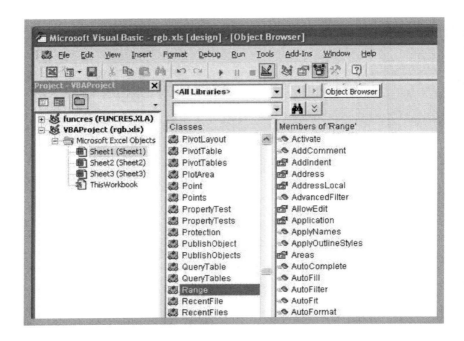

Object properties

Excel VBA object consists of properties and methods. Properties are characteristics or the attributes of an object. For example a range is an Excel VBA object with one of its properties being value. An object is connected to its property by a period or dot. The below example shows how to connect the property value with range object.

Private Sub CommandButton1_Click( )

Range("A1:A6").Value = 10

End Sub

Since the value is considered as a default property it can as well be omitted and the code can be written as;

Private Sub CommandButton1_Click( )

Range("A1:A6") = 10

End Sub

Cells are also Excel VBA objects and also the property of the range object. An object can be a property and it depends on the hierarchy of objects. The range has higher hierarchy than the cell and the interior with lower hierarchy than cells. Color also has lower hierarchy than the interior;

Range("A1:A3"). Cells(1,1).Interior.Color=vbYellow

This statement will fill the cells with yellow color and although the range object specifies a range from A1 to A3, the cells property specifies only the cells(1,1) to be filled with yellow color.

Another object is font and it belongs to the range object. Font also has its properties such as;

Range("A1:A4").Font.Color=vbYellow. The color property of object Font will result into all the contents from cell A1 to cell A4 to be filled with the yellow color.

It may not be necessary at times to type the properties as Excel VBA IntelliSence displays a drop-down list of the proposed properties once you type a period towards the end of the object name. You then select the property that you want by highlighting or double clicking on it then pressing the enter key.

Below is an example of IntelliSence drop-down;

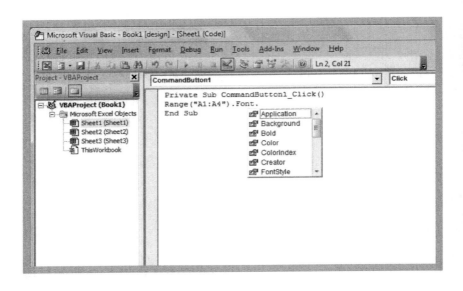

Chapter Three
PROGRAMMING CONCEPTS

Programming languages are somehow similar and having knowledge of what's common between them is critical for effective execution. It also enables one to transition easily from one language to another. There are two different models of programming;

Structured programming: In this type of programming, a code is executed one after another. The control statements change the block of codes that are executed. It is aimed at enhancing the quality, clarity and development time of a given computer program by making an extensive use of block structures, subroutines for while? loops.

Object-oriented programming: This type of programming is based on the concept of objects which contain data in the form of fields and often known as attributes and code. It's executed in the form of fields which are also referred to as methods. Object procedures access and modify data fields of a given object they're associated with. There is generally no actual flow as objects feely interact with each other by passing messages.

Here are some of the basic concepts of any programming language;

- Variables
- Program structures
- Control structures
- Looping structures
- Syntax

Variables

Variables are considered the backbone of any given programming language. A variable is considered as a storage location that's also associated with a symbolic name. It may contain a known or unknown quality of information that's referred to as value. The variable name is actually the usual way of referencing the stored value. In simple terms, a variable is a way of storing some information for later use. The information can refer to a word that describes the information.

Some of the different types of variables include;

Integer – Means to store whole numbers or integer

Real – Means to store real or even fractional numbers. It's also called float and indicates a floating point number.

Character – Refers to a single character like an alphabet letter or a punctuation.

String – Refers to a collection of characters.

```c
#include <stdio.h>
void main() {
    int age;
    float salary;
    char middle_initial;
    age = 25;
    salary = 196578.89;
    middle_initial = "K";
    printf("I am %d years old ", age);
    printf("I make %f per year " salary);
    printf("My middle initial is %c ", middle_initial);
}
```

Program Structures

Programs are normally referred to as well-structured or poorly-structured. A well-structured program has division into components that follows recognized principles such as hiding of information, and the interfaces of components are also simple and explicit. Poorly-structured program has division into components that is largely arbitrary and the interfaces are complex and explicit. A well-structured program utilizes appropriate data structures alongside program units that have a single exit point. Poorly-structured program on the other hand has arbitrary data structures alongside flow of control.

All of the structured programs share a similar pattern;

- Statements that establish the beginning of the program
- Variable declaration
- Program statements (blocks of code)

This is the basic example of "Hello world" that's used in all programming languages.

Control structures

A control structure generally is a block of programming that analyses the variables and chooses the direction in which it should go based on the provided parameters. Flow control expresses the direction taken by the program. It's therefore the decision-making process in computing. Flow control determines how a computer responds when provided with certain parameters and conditions. When a program is running, the code is read by the computer line after line. It can either be from top to bottom or left to right, in a similar way as reading a book. This is known as code flow.

As the computer reads the code, from top to bottom it may hit a place where it's required to make a decision. The decision might cause the code to shift to a different part of the program or a piece of code can be re-run or can also skip a bunch of code. The computer has set rules that are strict and helps in deciding the direction it should go. The decision made will affect the flow of code and is known as control structure.

Looping structures

Loop structures enable users to run lines of code repetitively. Users can repeat statements within a loop structure until the condition is considered as true or false a number of times. Below is a loop structure that runs a given set of statements until the condition is considered as true.

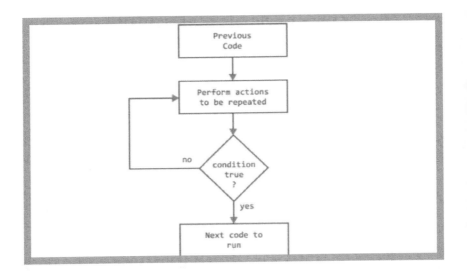

An infinite loop is that which lacks functioning exit routine. It then results into the loop, repeating several times until the operating system senses it and terminates the program with an error or until another event occurs.

Syntax

The syntax of programming language entails a set of rules that define a combination of symbols considered to be programs that are structured correctly in that language. The documents that are considered to be syntactically invalid are referred to as having a syntax error.

. . .

When a code has syntax errors, it becomes impossible for the program to execute. Programmers should therefore pay keen attention to detail in ensuring the code they write is free of syntax errors and also logical. There are several aspects to syntax such as variables, keywords and statements.

The computer language syntax is distinguished in three levels;

Words: Determines how characters form tokens

Phrases: Determines how the tokens form phrases. It also refers to grammar level.

Context: Determines objects or variables that names refer to and if the types are valid.

Chapter Four

ESSENTIAL VBA LANGUAGE ELEMENTS

VBA is a live programming language and uses several elements that are common to all programming languages. If you have programmed with other languages then you will find some of the elements to be quite familiar. The main function of VBA is to help with manipulating data. VBA stores data in the computer's memory and the data may either end up in the disk or not. Some of the data such as worksheet ranges resides in the objects while others are stored in the variables.

VBA programming Variables

A variable, as shared earlier, is a storage location within the computer's memory used by a program. Users have a lot of flexibility when it comes to naming variables, so the name used should be as descriptive as possible. A value is assigned to a variable through use of equal sign operator. Below is an example of variables that are being assigned values. The last example however uses two variables;

```
x = 1
InterestRate = 0.075
LoanPayoffAmount = 243089
DataEntered = False
x = x + 1
UserName = "Bob Johnson"
Date_Started = #3/14/2016#
MyNum = YourNum * 1.25
```

There are rules that are enforced by VBA regarding variable names;

- You can use numbers, letters and even punctuation characters, however the first character must be a letter.
- VBA doesn't actually distinguish between letters written in uppercase and lowercase.
- Avoid using many spaces, mathematical operators or periods in a variable name.
- The following characters cannot be used in a variable name; #, $, %, & and !

- Variable names should not be longer than 255 characters although nobody ever gets close to the limit.

For the variable names to be readable, programmers normally use a mixed case such as InterestRate or the underscore character (interest_rate).

VBA has several reserved words that cannot be used as variable names or even procedure names. These are words such as Sub, With, Dim, End, For and Next. Any attempt to use any of the words as a variable leads to error which means that the code may not run. So if a statement produces an error message then you should double check to make sure that the variable name used is not a reserved word.

You can do that by selecting the variable name then pressing on F1 and if the name is of a reserved word it will have an entry within the Help system. VBA enables users to create variables with names that match with those in Excel's object model such as Range and Workbook.

However use of such names may only increase the possibility of confusion. For example; Macro that declares the range as a variable name also works with a cell named range within a worksheet named range and that can be valid yet very confusing.

```
Sub RangeConfusion()
    Dim Range As Double
    Range = Sheets("Range").Range("Range").Value
    MsgBox Range
End Sub
```

Programmers should therefore resist the use of a variable named as Workbook or Range and instead go for something like MyWorkbook or MyRange.

Chapter Five

VBA DATA TYPES

Data types entail the manner in which a program stores data within a memory such as integers, strings or real numbers. As much as VBA can take care of the details automatically; it however does that at a cost. Allowing VBA to handle the data typing leads to inefficient use of memory and slower execution. It may not present many problems for smaller applications however for large and complex applications it may be much slower.

If you are to conserve every memory byte then you should be familiar with data types. The fact that VBA handles all the details of data automatically makes the process much easier for programmers and not all of the programming languages provide this possibility. Some languages are strictly typed which means that the programmer has to define type of data for every variable used.

VBA doesn't require that programmers declare the variables although it's good practice. There are a variety of built-in data types in VBA and below are some of the common types of data that can be handled by VBA.

Data Type
    Bytes Used
    Range of Values
    Byte
    1
    0 to 255
    Boolean
    2
    True or False
    Integer
    2
    -32,768 to 32,767
    Long
    4
    -2,147,483,648 to 2, 147,483,647
    Single
    4
    13,40E38 to -1.40E-45 for negative values
    1.40E-45 to 3.40E38 for positive values
    Double
    8
    -1.79E308 to -4.94E-324 for negative values;
    4.94E-324 to 1.79E308 for positive values
    Currency
    8
    -922,338,203,685,477 to
    922,337,203,685,477

Date
8
1/1/0100 to 12/31/9999
Object
4
Any object reference
String
1 per
Character
Varies
Variant
Varies
Varies

Consider choosing a data type that uses the smallest number of bytes and is still capable of handling all the data you intend to store in the variable.

SCOPING AND DECLARING VARIABLES

If you fail to declare the data type for a given variable that you are using in a VBA routine, the VBA may use a default data type which is variant. Data stored as a variant keeps changing its type depending on whatever you do with it.

For example, if a variable is a variant data type and has a text string that looks more like a number then you can use the variable for numeric calculations and also for string manipulation. VBA handles the conversion automatically.

Allowing VBA to handle the data types may look like an easy way out however be aware of the fact that you are sacrificing speed and also increasing memory used. Before using variables in a procedure, it's ideal to declare the variables by notifying VBA of each of the variable's data type.

Declaring the variables makes the macros run much faster with efficient use of memory. The default data type, variant makes VBA perform time consuming checks repeatedly and also reserve more memory than actually necessary.

If VBA is aware of a variable's data type then it doesn't have to spend time investigating and is then capable of reserving sufficient memory for storing the data. To force declaration of the variables that you use, include the two words as the first statement in the VBA module, (Option Explicit). When this statement is noticed you may not be able to run your code at all if it contains undeclared variables.

Option Explicit should only be used once and at the beginning of your module before you declare any procedures within the module. Remember that the statement only applies to the module in which it resides. In case you have more than one module within a project then you need an Option Explicit statement for each of the modules.

To ensure that Option Explicit statement is automatically inserted when you insert a new VBA module then you need to turn the Require Variable Definition Option on. You can find it on the editor tab within the options dialog box in the VBE, choose tools>options.

Declaring of variables also enables users to take advantage of shortcut. You can do that by typing the first two or three characters of the variable name then press Ctrl+ Space bar.

The VBE will complete the entry and in case the choice is ambiguous, you will be shown a list of matching words to choose from. You can declare variables by using Dim statement. Below are some of the declared variables;

```
Dim YourName As String
Dim January_Inventory As Double
Dim AmountDue As Double
Dim RowNumber As Long
Dim X
```

The first four variables have been declared as specific data type. The last variable X is however not declared as specific data type. Therefore it's treated as a variant which means it can actually be anything. Apart from Dim, there are other keywords that can be used to declare variables; Static, Public and Private.

. . .

A workbook can have several VBA modules and a VBA module can equally have any given number of Sub and Function procedures.

The scope of a variable helps in determining which of the modules and procedures can make use of the variable.

WORKING WITH CONSTANTS

A variable value is likely to change while your procedure is being executed. Constants are declared by using Const statement and the declaration statement gives the constant its value.

```
Const NumQuarters As Integer = 4
Const Rate = .0725, Period = 12
Const ModName As String = "Budget Macros"
Public Const AppName As String = "Budget Application"
```

Use of constants instead of the hard-coded strings or values is a great programming practice. For example, if your procedure is to refer to a specific value like an interest rate, then it's ideal to declare your code in a way that's more readable and easier to change.

Just like variables, constants have a scope so keep the following in mind;

- To make a constant available in a single procedure, you need to declare the constant right after the procedure's Sub and Function statement.
- To make constant available to all of the procedures within a module, you should declare the constant at the declarations section for the module.
- To make a constant available to all of the modules within a workbook, remember to use Public keyword then declare the constant within the declarations section of any of the module.

The value of a constant doesn't vary unlike that of a variable. In case you attempt to change the value of a constant within a VBA routine then you will get an error. The value of a constant should remain constant and if you want to change the value while the code is running then you need a variable.

Excel and VBA have many predefined constants which can be used without having to declare them.

The macro recorder normally uses constants instead of the actual values. It's great to know that you don't have to be aware of the value of the constants in order to use them.

STRING AND STRING FUNCTIONS

A string refers to a sequence of characters that include numbers, alphabetical and special characters in combination. Excel is capable of working with both the numbers and text and VBA has the same power.

Text is also referred to as a string and you can work with two types of strings in VBA. A variable is considered to be a string if its value is enclosed using double quotes.

Fixed-length strings: These are declared with a given number of characters. The maximum length should be 65,526 characters which is a lot of characters.

Variable-length strings: These are capable of theoretically holding as many characters as possible even up to two billion. If you type about 5 characters per second then it may take 760 days to write the 2 billion characters and that's assuming you don't take a break.

Excel is capable of handling strings and also the standalone VBA program.

All of the string handling functions in VBA are Len, Mid, Trim, Ltrim, Rtrim, Right, Left, Ucase, Lcase, Instr, Chr, Str, and Asc. All of these functions can be used in Excel VBA.

The Instr Function

This is a function that looks for and also returns the position of the substring into a phrase.

For example;

```
Private Sub cmdlInstr_Click ()
Dim Phrase As String
Phrase = Cells(1,1). Value
Cells(4,1)=InStr(phrase, "ual")
End Sub
```

The function InsStr(phrase,"ual") will find the substring "ual" from the phrase "Visual Basic" entered in the cells (1,1) then return its position which in this case is 4 from the left.

The Left Function

This is a function that extracts characters from a phrase beginning from the left. Left(phrase,4) means 4 characters are extracted from the specific phrase beginning from the left most position. For example;

```
Private Sub cmdLeft_Click()
Dim phrase As String
Phrase = Cells(1,1). Value
Cells(2,1) = Left(phrase,4)
End Sub
```

This code returns substring "Visu" from the phrase "Visual Basic" entered in the cells (1,1)

The Right Function

This function extracts characters from a phrase beginning from the Right.Right(phrase,5) which means 5 characters are extracted from the phrase beginning from the right most position. For example;

```
Private Sub cmdRight_Click()
Dim phrase As String
Phrase = Cells (1,1). Value
Cells(3,1) = Right (phrase,5)
End Sub
```

This code is used in returning the substring "Basic" from the phrase "Visual Basic" which is entered in cells (1,1)

The Mid Function

This is a function that extracts a substring from a given phrase beginning from the position that's specified by the second parameter within the bracket.

Mid(phrase,8,3) means that a substring of 3 characters are extracted from the specified phrase beginning from the 8th position right from the left including the empty space.

```
Private Sub cmdMid_Click()
Dim phrase As String
Phrase = Cells (1, 1). Value
Cells(5,1) = Mid(phrase, 8, 3)
End Sub
```

This code returns substring "Bas" from the phrase "Visual Basic" as entered in cells(1,1)

The Len Function

This function returns the length of a given phase including the empty space that exists between. For example;

```
Private Sub cmdLen_Click()
Dim phrase As String
Phrase = Cells(1,1). Value
Cells(6,1) = Len (phrase)
```

The code then returns 12 for the phrase "Visual Basic" which is entered in the cells as (1, 1)

Visual Basic Editor in Microsoft Excel is capable of handling strings as a standalone VB program. All the string handling functions in Visual Basic like Left, Right, Instr, Len and Midcan may be used within Visual Basic Editor.

The Ucase and Lcase Functions

Ucase function converts all of the characters of a string into capital letters. Lcase function on the other hand converts all of the characters of a string into small letters. For example;

Ucase("excelvba") =EXCEL VBA

Lcase("Excel VBA") = excel vba.

The Str and Val Functions

Str function converts a number to a string and Val function converts a string to a number. Both of the functions are very important when required to perform mathematical operations.

The Chr and Asc Functions

Chr function returns the string in a way that corresponds to ASCII code while Asc function converts ASCII character or symbol to a corresponding ASCII code. ASCII refers to American Standard Code for Information Interchange and there are up to 255 ASCII codes with many ASCII characters. Some of the characters might not be displayed as they represent actions like the pressing of a key. Format for Chr function is

Chr(charcode)
    And the format of Asc function
    Asc (character)
    Below is an example'
    Chr(65)=A, Chr(122)=z, Chr(37)=%,ASC("B")=66, Asc("&")=38

CONTROLLING PROGRAM FLOW AND MAKING DECISIONS

A control structure refers to a combination of keywords within a code that's used in making decisions having the potential of altering the flow of code the computer executes.

Controlling program flow and decision-making is a very important part in Excel VBA. Problems can be intelligently solved and useful feedback attained that helps users.

Some of the VBA procedures start at the beginning of the code and continues to progress line-by-line up to the end without deviating from the top-to bottom program flow. Macros that users record normally work this way.

Users need to control the flow of their code by skipping over some of the statements, executing some of the statements several times and also testing conditions in order to determine what the procedure does.

Some beginners may find it hard understanding how a computer is capable of making intelligent decisions. The secret however lies in several programming constructs supported by several programming languages.

The below table below provide a quick summary of the constructs.

Constructs and How it works

GoTo statement
　Jumps to a particular statement

If-Then structure
Does something if something else is true

Select Case
Does any of several things, depending on something's value.

For-Next loop
Executes a series of statements a specified number of times

Do-While loop
Does something as long as something else remains true

Do-Until loop
Does something until something else becomes true

The GoTo Statement: This offers a straightforward way of changing the flow of a program. The GoTo statement helps in transferring the execution of a program to a new statement which is preceded by a label.

VBA routines can have as many labels as preferred. A label is actually a text string followed by a colon. Below is an example of how the GoTo statement works;

```
Sub CheckUser()

    UserName = InputBox("Enter Your Name: ")

    If UserName <> "Steve Ballmer" Then GoTo WrongName

    MsgBox ("Welcome Steve...")

'   ...[More code here] ...

    Exit Sub
WrongName:
    MsgBox "Sorry. Only Steve Ballmer can run this."

End Sub
```

The procedure uses Input Box function to access the user's name. A decision is then made and if the user enters a wrong name then the program flow jumps to the Wrong Name label. It also displays an apology message and the procedures immediately end.

If the user runs the macro and uses the correct name then the procedure will display a welcome message and also execute some additional code.

These simple routines work well however VBA tends to provide other better and more structured alternatives. GoTo should only be used when there is no other way to perform an action. GoTo can only be used when trapping errors.

Decisions

Decision making enables programmers to take control of the

execution flow of a script or one of its sections. The execution process is governed by one or several conditional statements.

Effective decision making is vital when writing Excel macros. A successful Excel application entails making decisions and acting upon them effectively. Below is a form of typical decision making structure that's found in several programming languages.

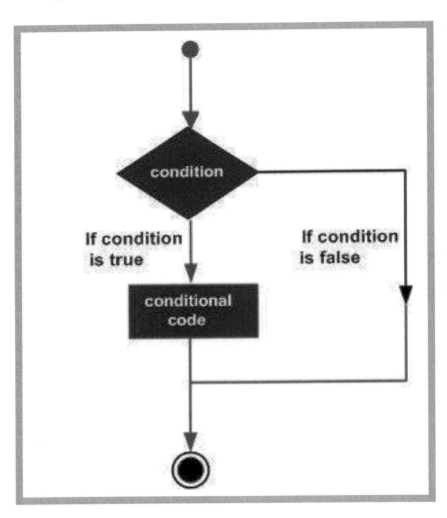

VBA provides users with the following types of decision making statements.

Statement & Description

If statement

It consists of a Boolean expression which is followed by one statement or more.

If..else

If else statement also consists of a Boolean expression which is then followed by one or more statements. If in case the condition is true then the statement under if are executed. If the condition is false then the else part of the script is executed.

If..elseif..else

An if statement that's followed by one or several elseif statements consists of Boolean expressions. It's then followed by another optional else statement which executes when all the conditions turn out as fault.

If or elseif

If or elseif statement inside another if and elseif statement.

Switch

Switch statement enables the testing of a variable equality against a list of values.

. . .

There are programming structures that users can make use of to empower VBA procedures with some of the impressive decision making capabilities. There is the If-Then and Select Case.

The If-Then Structure

If-Then is one of the most important control structures in VBA. This is a command that programmers will use on a daily basis. Decision making normally involves use of IF ..then..Else syntax that are used in processing data and displaying the output based on fulfillment of specific conditions.

For users to effectively control the flow of VB program, If..then..Else statements can be used together with logical and conditional operators. You can make use of the If-Then structure whenever you want to execute one or several statements conditionally.

The first control structure that users need to know is If... Then. The syntax for this structure is shown as;

```
If condition = True Then
    ...the code that executes if the condition is satisfied
End If
```

If the condition is true then the code in the If and End If statement is executed. If the condition is not true then the code within the statements is skipped and not executed.

If..Then..Else structure is applied if you want to do one thing if the prevailing condition is true and another thing if the condition is not true. If the optional Else clause is included and enables one to execute one or more of the statements if the condition being tested is not true. Below is an example of If-Then-else structure;

```
If condition = True Then
    ...this is the code that executes if the condition is satisfied
Else
    ...this is the code that executes if the condition is not satisfied
End If
```

The below routine demonstrates If-Then structure without the Else clause:

```
Sub GreetMe()

    If Time < 0.5 Then MsgBox "Good Morning"

End Sub
```

GreetMe procedures on the other hand use VBA'a time function to attain the system time. If the time is lower than .5 or before noon then it displays a friendly greeting. If time is greater than or equal to .5 then user's can add another If-Then statement right after the first one.

```
Sub GreetMe2()

    If Time < 0.5 Then MsgBox "Good Morning"

    If Time >= 0.5 Then MsgBox "Good Afternoon"

End Sub
```

Select Case Structure

If you have to perform a large number of tests with the same expression then select statement enables your code to read and interpret in a much easier way than would have been with a long list of If..then and If..then..Else statements. Select case structure is therefore defined as follows;

```
Select Case test_expression
    Case expression-1
        ...this is the code that executes if expression-1 matches test_expression
    Case expression-2
        ...this is the code that executes if expression-2 matches test_expression
    Case expression-3
        ...this is the code that executes if expression-3 matches test_expression
    Case Else
        ...this is the code that executes if expression-n matches test_expression
End Select
```

Conditional Logic

In programming, specific sections of the code are executed depending on the results of one or several conditions. In order to check, a series of keywords and operators that can be combined are availed. When the conditions are checked it produces a true or false result depending on the statements. If—then is a logic that's formed by two words or facts. It means saying what has to happen if a given condition is met.

Programming Loops

Situations might arise where you need to execute a block of code several times. Statements are generally executed sequentially with the first statement in a function being the first to be executed followed by the rest. Programming languages normally provide several control structures that make it possible for more complicated execution paths.

A loop statement enables users to execute a statement or groups of statements several times. Loop control statements are used to change execution from the normal sequence. When execution leaves a scope, the remaining statements in the loop aren't executed.

Loop type & Description

For loop
Executes a range of statements several times and also abbreviates the code used in managing the loop variable.

For..each loop
This gets executed if there is at least one element within the group and it's reiterated for each of the elements within the group.

While..wend loop
This tests conditions before the loop body is executed.

. . .

Do..while loops

The do,..while statements can be executed as long as the given condition is true. The loop should then be repeated until the condition is false.

Do..until loops

This will be executed as long as the given condition is false. The loop should therefore be repeated until the condition becomes true.

∼

PROGRAMMING ARRAYS

Arrays are variables that enable users to store more than a value into a single variable. A specific element within the array can be referred to by using the array name and index number. Each value within the array is referred to as an element.

Since an array variable has several elements within it, users need a way to pick out or reference them individually and that can be done by use of a number referred to as index.

In most cases, the first element of an array is index number 0. An array index begins from 0 by default and this can be changed through use of option base.

Chapter Six

VBA SUB AND FUNCTION PROCEDURES

If you are to have good understanding of Excel VBA then it's advisable to have a good grasp of the concept of procedures, the various types of procedures and how you can work with them.

When using Visual Basic Editor in Excel, a procedure refers to the block of statements enclosed by a specific declaration and end declaration.

VBA instructions are normally within procedure so to master VBA and macros then familiarity with this topic is critical. There are two common types of procedures in VBA; the sub procedures and function procedures.

The main difference between VBA sub procedures and function procedures lies in the following;

- VBA Sub procedures are used in performing an action within Excel. For example, when a VBA sub procedure is executed, Excel does something. Whatever happens in Excel depends on what the specific VBA code says.

- Function procedures on the other hand execute calculations and then return a value. The value can either be a single value or an array. Function procedures work in a similar way as Excel functions. They execute specific calculations behind the scenes then return the values.

- Most of the macros written in VBA are actually sub procedures. If you use macro recorder for creating a macro then Excel will always create a VA sub procedure.

A VBA Sub procedure begins with a declaration statement such as "Sub" and has an end declaration statement. It also has a block of statements enclosed by a start declaration and end declaration statement.

```
Sub Delete_Blank_Rows_3()
'
' Delete_Blank_Rows_3 Macro
' Deletes rows when cells within the row are blank.
'
' Keyboard Shortcut: Ctrl+Shift+B
'
    On Error Resume Next
    Selection.EntireRow.SpecialCells(xlBlanks).EntireRow.Delete
    On Error GoTo 0

End Sub
```

The main purpose of this VBA procedure; "Delete_Blank_Rows_3" is to delete rows when some of the cells within the rows are blank. There are 3 items in the statement. It has the Sub keyword which is used to declare the beginning of the sub procedure.

It has the name of the VBA sub procedure which must follow certain rules. It also has parentheses. When you're creating VBA sub procedures that use arguments from other procedures then the argument should be separated with a comma (,).

If the procedures have no arguments then you should have a set of empty parentheses. There are 4 elements that are required in any of the VBA procedure;

- Sub statement
- Name
- Parenthesis
- End Sub keyword.

VBA FUNCTION PROCEDURES

The data types determine how data is stored in the computer memory. An inadequate use of VBA data types normally leads into inefficient use of memory and may have diverse effects in practice.

It may lead to slower execution of the VBA applications where data types might be used incorrectly.

VBA Function procedure returns different types of data types and users can choose the particular data type that is returned by a function procedure. When declaring arguments for a VBA function, users can use a keyword and Type statement for the purpose of determining the data type.

Users should ensure that the data type of the specific argument matches the expected data type by the relevant procedure.

Unlike execution of a VBA sub procedure, the options for executing VBA Function procedure are quite restricted. Users cannot execute VBA Function procedure directly through use of the same methods as those of Sub procedure.

Function procedure can be executed in the following 3 ways;

- It can be executed by calling it from another procedure and the calling procedure can be a Sub procedure of Function procedure.

- It can be executed by calling it from Visual Basic Editor immediate window.

- It can also be executed by using it in a formula like a worksheet formula or a formula used for specifying conditional formatting.

USING THE EXCEL MACRO RECORDER

The macro recorder is such a vital tool in Excel VBA which records all of the tasks that are performed in Excel. All users need to do is record a given task once and the task can be executed over and over just with the click of a button.

Macro recorder also acts as a great source of help when one doesn't know how to have a specific task programmed in Excel VBA.

All you have to do is open the visual basic editor after recording the given task then view how it can be programmed. There are however some tasks that cannot be done with macro recorder.

For example, you may not be able to loop through a range of data within the macro recorder. The macro recorder also uses more code than required and that can slow down the process.

. . .

To automate tasks that are repetitive, users can record a macro by applying the format required for a given task. The macro can then be replayed when desired. When recording a macro, all of the steps are recorded in the VBA code.

The steps include; typing numbers or texts, clicking commands or cells on the menus or ribbon, formatting of cells, and even importing data from an external source.

VBA is a subset of a powerful programming language and provides users with the ability to automate processes within Excel and between Office applications. Since the macro recorder captures every step, you should re-record the entire sequence in case you make a mistake.

Writing and Recording macros

The VBA tools are available on the Developer tab which is normally hidden by default. So you need to enable it as you get started.

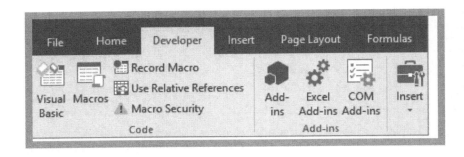

To record a macro, get to the developer tab then click on record macro. You can also press Alt+T+M+R

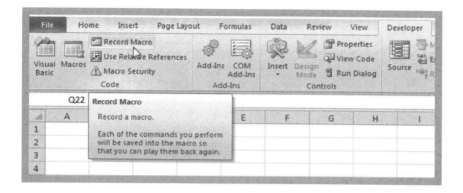

The next step is to enter a name by selecting this workbook from the drop down list. The macro will then be available only in the current workbook.

In the macro name box, enter the macro name and make it with as much description as you can. The character of the macro name should be a letter and the subsequent ones can either be a letter, numbers or even underscore characters.

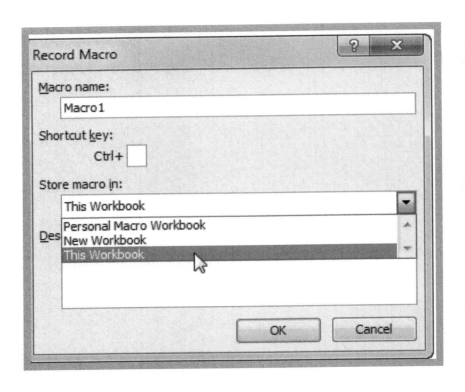

In the store macro list, select where you want to store the macro. If you store the macro into personal macro workbook then it will be available to all Excel files. This is possible since Excel stores macros in a hidden workbook that opens automatically whenever Excel starts.

If you store the macros in a new workbook then it will be available in an automatically opened new workbook. You can then click ok.

You can then right click on an active cell then select format cells. Select on percentage then click ok. Finally, click on stop recording;

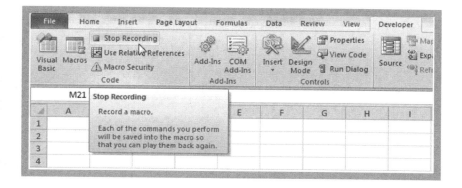

To run a recorded macro, you can test the macro to check if the number format will change to percentage. Enter some of the numbers between 0 – 1 then select the numbers. On the developer tab click on the macros then click on run.

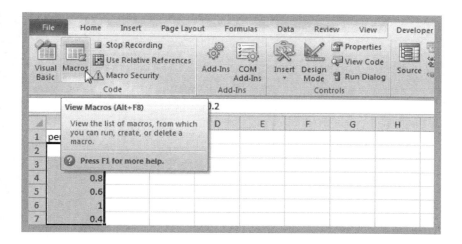

The result will look as below;

	A	B
1	percentages	
2	20.00%	
3	60.00%	
4	80.00%	
5	60.00%	
6	100.00%	
7	40.00%	
8		

To have a look at the macro, open the visual basic editor and notice that it has been placed into a module known as Module 1. The code placed in the module is available for use in the whole workbook.

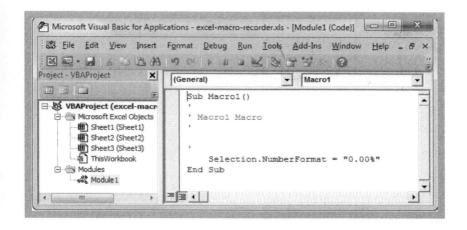

To work with recorded macros in Excel, go to the developer tab then click on macros. You will be able to view macros that are associated to a workbook. You can also press Alt + F8 and a macro dialog box will open.

You can work with the recorded code in the visual basic editor then add your own control structures, variables and other code that the macro recorder may not be able to record.

AUTOMATIC PROCEDURES AND EVENTS

Once you have created a macro, you will need a way to execute it or even call it. There are several options within Excel that can be used for calling or running a VBA sub procedure.

A useful way of executing a macro is by informing Excel that a specific procedure should be executed when a given occurs. Having knowledge on how to do this allows one to create VBA applications that are capable of doing things that would be impossible.

Excel VBA events takes place while you are working in Excel. Events are considered to be useful since it enables one to create macros that can be executed automatically when a specific event occurs.

It therefore allows one to add interactivity to Excel workbooks, improve user experience and also be able to perform activities that would be impossible to execute without VBA events.

The sub procedures that are executed automatically when a specific event occurs are also referred to as event handler procedures.

Events can be classified into the following categories;

Application events: Occurs in Excel application itself.

Workbook events: Happens whenever something happens to a workbook.

Worksheet events: Are triggered whenever something takes place in a worksheet.

Chart events: Occurs whenever something happens to a chart.

. . .

UserForm events: happens to a user form or an object that exists within a user form.

Non-object events: Are not associated with any particular object. This type of event works differently from the other categories. These events can be accessed through VBA methods of application object.

WORKING WITH VBA SUB PROCEDURES

The fastest way to execute a VBA procedure is by running it directly through a Visual Basic Editor. Normally, you may want to execute VBA procedures while in Excel and not in the VBE.

This method works when the specific VBA sub procedure that you intend to run doesn't rely on arguments that are from another procedure. The reason being that this option doesn't allow users to pass arguments from other procedures to the VBA sub procedure that you may be calling.

If you intend to run a VBA that has arguments then the only way to do it is by calling it from another procedure. The procedure you are calling from should then supply the arguments that are required by the sub procedure that you intend to execute.

To execute the VBA sub procedure; begin by opening the Visual Basic Editor then open VBA module that that you intend to execute as the VBA sub procedure. The Visual Basic Editor should be able to show you the VBA code for the sub procedure that you intend to call.

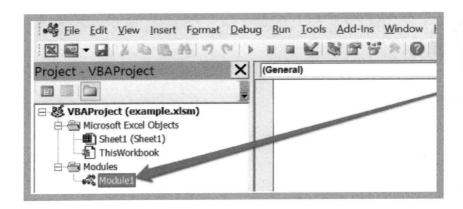

The Visual Basic Editor will then be able to display the relevant code within the programming window.

```
Sub Delete_Blank_Rows_3()
'
' Delete_Blank_Rows_3 Macro
' Deletes rows when cells within the row are blank.
'
' Keyboard Shortcut: Ctrl+Shift+B
'
    On Error Resume Next
    Selection.EntireRow.SpecialCells(xlBlanks).EntireRow.Delete
    On Error GoTo 0
End Sub
```

You can then call the VBA procedure directly from the relevant module by using the below methods. Over Run menu, click on Run Sub/UserForm. You can also use F5 as keyboard shortcut.

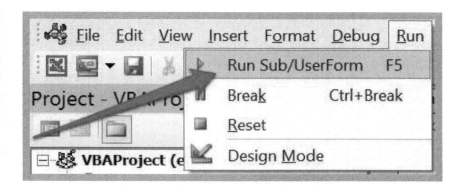

The second option for executing a VBA sub procedure is through use of the macro dialog. This method works well if the VBA procedure you intend to call doesn't contain arguments. This option is one of the commonly used methods for executing VBA sub procedures.

You can begin by opening the macro dialog by either using keyboard shortcut; "Alt + F8. You can also click on macros over the developer tab of the ribbon.

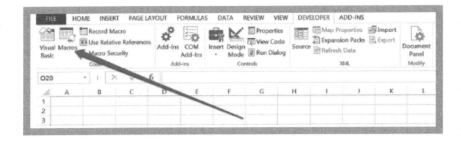

You can then select the macro you intend to execute. According to the sample below, there is only one macro open (Delete_Blank_Rows_3). It's therefore the only macro that will be executed.

You can then double click on the macro that you intend to execute, then click on run. It's also possible to execute a VBA sub procedure by using a keyboard shortcut. All you have to do to run a macro is to press the relevant key combinations.

Do that by selecting the VBA sub procedure that you intend to assign a macro to then click on options. Go ahead and assign a keyboard shortcut then click on OK button. The keyboard shortcuts are Ctrl + letter or Ctrl + Shift + Letter.

When assigning the keyboard shortcut, you should be keen on the combination that you are assigning to the VBA procedure.

CREATING FUNCTION PROCEDURES

Excel VBA function procedures take arguments and also return values. The VBA functions are quite versatile and can be used when working with VBA or in an Excel worksheet formula.

There are over four hundred Excel functions with a huge range of calculations however some are more useful than others.

VBA function procedures help in simplifying work and can be used for shortening formulas. Shorter formulas are much easier to read and understand.

Custom functions may help with creation of application by reducing duplication of code which in turn minimizes errors.

VBA functions can also be used to execute operations that may otherwise look impossible.

VBA procedures can also be of great help when creating VBA projects that are quite large and complex. Since VBA functions take incoming data and return values that result from the calculations, they are quite useful for helping the different procedures communicate between themselves. One of the main reasons for creating and using VBA function procedures is the main purpose of improving your VBA coding skills.

When creating function procedures, you can make use of the macro recorder and you should ensure that you enter the appropriate VBA code.

Some of the basic elements for VBA function procedure are;

- Always starts with the function keyword.
- Always ends with the End Function statement.
- Contains a relevant block of statements alongside instructions between declarations and end statements.

Function Squared (number)
Squared = number ^ 2
End Function

The function keyword that declares the start of VBA function is <u>Function</u> Squared (number)

The name of the VBA function procedure is Squared.

Function Squared (number)

The arguments that have been taken by the function are enclosed by parentheses. According to the above example, the Squared function only takes 1 argument: number.

Function Squared (number)

This VBA function procedure takes several arguments and a comma is used to separate them (,). If you are creating a function that doesn't make arguments then consider leaving the parentheses empty. Remember that you should always include the parentheses even if they are empty.

Naming of Excel VBA Function Procedures

The function names are expected to adhere to the variable names. When naming variables, the name should start with letters. The names can also include numbers, punctuation characters such as underscore.

The maximum number of characters should be up to 255 and there are no spaces allowed as names should be a continuous string of characters only.

When naming the VBA procedures, remember not to use function names that match with a named range or cell reference such as A1. If you do that then you will not be able to use that specific VBA function in a worksheet formula. If you try it then excel will show it as an error.

Avoid using VBA function procedure names that are similar to that of built in functions like SUM. This may cause a name conflict between the functions and Excel tends to use the built-in function instead of the created VBA function.

Arguments are the data or information used as an input by function in order to carry out calculations. When working with function procedures arguments will be encountered in the following situations;

When declaring a VBA function procedure, users should also include arguments that are taken by the function. If the function takes no arguments then you can just leave the parentheses empty. The above example only takes 1 argument.

To create function procedures with an indefinite number of arguments; use as the only argument in the list of arguments that also include the declaration statement of VBA function. You can also use ParamArray keyword prior to the final array argument. According to the above example, the VBA function procedure which is referred to as Squared_Sum. You can see how arguments are declared as an array of elements of a variant data type;

```
Function Squared_Sum(ParamArray arglist() As Variant) As Double
    Dim cell As Range
    For Each arg In arglist
        For Each cell In arg
            Squared_Sum = Squared_Sum + (cell ^ 2)
        Next cell
    Next arg
End Function
```

The above VBA function procedure is not flexible and might fail when a range of cells are used as argument and one of the cells has a string instead of a number.

Chapter Seven

INTRODUCING THE EXCEL OBJECT MODEL

The object Model

Excel VBA is mainly based around object oriented programming concept. The secret to successfully using VBA with other applications lies in having a good understanding of the object model for each of the applications.

VBA involves manipulation of objects and each of the office products has its unique object model.

The object model is a hierarchy of all the objects that are used in VBA. The hierarchy makes referencing of VBA objects to be much easier.

The hierarchy looks like below;

- Have one single object at the very top.

- The object that's at the top of the hierarchy contains some objects.
- Those in the second level of the hierarchy may also contain more objects.
- The objects in the third level may also contain other objects.
- The process is repeated until you reach an object that doesn't contain other objects.

If you are working with a given application, the application object remains at the top of the hierarchy and the application is therefore Excel itself. The application object also has other VBA objects such as

- Add-Ins – contains all of the add-in objects.
- Windows – contains all of the window objects within the application.
- Workbooks – contains all of the workbook objects.

The VBA objects also contain other objects. For example; objects contained in the workbook are the following;

- Charts which also contain chart objects.
- Names which contains name objects
- VBProjects which represents the open objects.
- Windows which also contain the window objects within Excel workbook.
- Worksheets also contain worksheet objects.

These VBA objects may also contain other objects such as;

- Chart objects contains chart object objects
- Comment represents a cell comment
- Hyperlink represents hyperlink
- Name represents a defined name for a given cell range.
- PageSetup used for storing information
- PivotTables contains PivotTable objects.
- Range represents cells, columns, rows, and selection of cells with 3-d ranges or continuous block of cells.

Here is an overview of how the hierarchy looks;

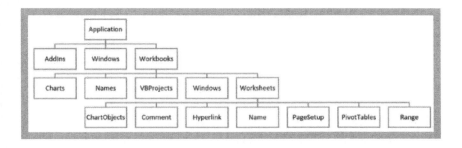

Developers normally organize programming objects into a hierarchy which is referred to as object model of application.

An object is referred to in VBA code that's specifying its position in the hierarchy of objects. Objects are separated by a period (.) separator for example, a workbook that's named as

Expenses.xlsx can be referred to as Application.Workbooks("Expenses.xlsx").

This expresses that "Expenses.xlsx" workbook is one of the workbooks within the collection of workbooks. Workbooks collection is found in the Application object in Excel and you can refer to Sheet1 in "Expenses.xlsx" workbook as follows;

Application.Workbooks("Expenses.xlsx").Worksheets("Sheets1")

Objects have properties and a property is a setting for an object. For example; a range object has several properties such as value and address. A chart may also have a type, title and many other settings. These settings are the properties of chart objects but may be have a different name. The VBA can be used to change the values of properties. Objects can be combined with properties and separated by a period (.) Values can also be assigned to variables and a variable is an element of VBA that stores text or value.

Objects have methods which can be used to perform specific tasks with the object. Methods are of both types and are built-in and customized. For example; the range object has ClearContents as a built-in method. This method helps in clearing the range contents. Objects can be combined with methods by separating them using a period (.) To clear contents for the range E11:F20, you can use the following VBA statement;

Worksheets("Sheet1").Range("E11:F20").ClearContents.

VBA also includes all the constructs of the modern programming languages including the typed variables, looping, arrays, and debugging aids amongst others.

Chapter Eight
ERROR-HANDLING TECHNIQUES

When working with Excel VBA, you need to be aware of the two broad classes of errors. There are the programming errors which are also known as bugs and runtime errors.

A well written program has the potential of handling errors carefully and in Excel VBA, there are several tools that can help with identification of errors.

Handling of errors refers to use of a code written to handle errors. The errors are generally caused by something beyond control such as a missing file, data being invalid or a database being unavailable. If a user expects an error to occur at a given point then it's advisable that a specific code be written to handle the error. For all other errors, a generic code is normally used to deal with them.

. . .

VBA error handling statement allows the application to handle errors that were not expected. To understand how to handle the errors, one needs to have a clear understanding of the different types of errors in VBA.

∼

VBA ERROR TYPES

There are three different types of errors in Excel VBA. There are the syntax errors, runtime and compilation errors.

Syntax errors

If you have used Excel VBA for some time then you have definitely come across syntax errors. When you type a statement and press on return, the VBA evaluates the syntax and if it's not correct, an error message is displayed. For example if you type If but forget to include then keyword, VBA will then display an error message like the one below;

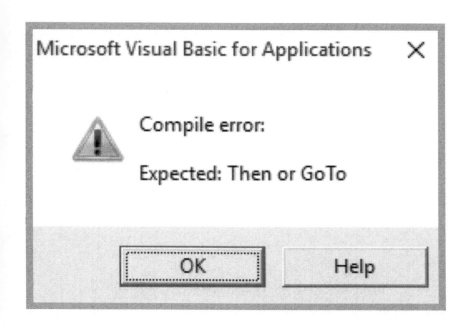

Other examples of syntax errors include;

```
' then is missing
If a > b


' equals is missing after i
For i 2 To 7


' missing right parenthesis
b = left("ABCD",1
```

Syntax relates only to one line and the errors occur if the syntax of a specific line is incorrect. Syntax error dialog can be turned off by going to Tools>Options then checking off the auto syntax check.

Compilation errors

Compilation errors occur with more than a line. The syntax maybe correct in one line but incorrect in another. Examples of compilation errors include;

- Use of an If statement without inclusion of End if statement.
- Use of For without Next
- Use of Select without End Select
- Calling of a Sub or Function that doesn't exist
- Calling of a Sub or Function with wrong parameters.
- Giving Sub or Function the same name as that of a module.

Below example shows compilation error that occurs when For loop lacks a matching Next statement.

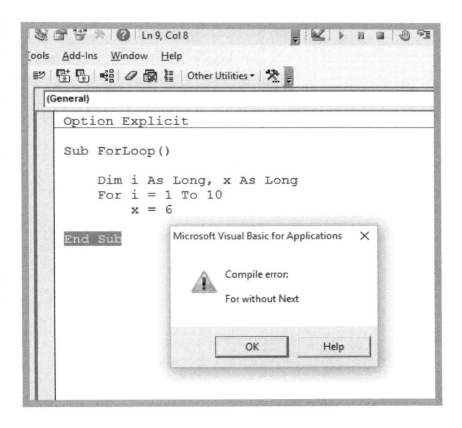

To find compilation errors use Debug>Compile VBA project from the Visual Basic menu. When you select Debug>Compile, VBA then displays the first error that it comes across. Once the error has been fixed, you can again run Compile and the VBA will find the next error.

Debug>Compile also includes syntax errors within its search which is quite useful. When there are no errors left and you continue to run Debug>Compile, nothing may appear but Compile will be grayed out from the Debug menu. It therefore means that your application doesn't have any more errors at the specific time.

Runtime Errors

Runtime errors normally occur when the application is running. These errors are normally out of the user's control and can also be caused by errors within the code. Examples of runtime errors are;

- Unavailable database
- Entry of an invalid data by a user
- Cell containing text instead of a number

The purpose of error handling is to deal with the runtime errors whenever they occur. The below code can be used to check if the specific file exists before one tries to open it. If the file doesn't exist, a user friendly message will then be displayed as the code exits the sub.

```vb
Sub OpenFile()

    Dim sFile As String
    sFile = "C:\docs\data.xlsx"

    ' Use Dir to check if file exists
    If Dir(sFile) = "" Then
        ' if file does not exist display message
        MsgBox "Could not find the file " & sFile
        Exit Sub
    End If

    ' Code will only reach here if file exists
    Workbooks.Open sFile

End Sub
```

When you suspect an error might occur at some point, it's advisable to add code to help in handling the situation. Such errors are referred to as expected errors. If you don't have a specific code to handle the errors then it can be referred to as unexpected errors. VBA error handling statements are therefore used for handling the unexpected errors.

On Error Goto 0

This is VBA's default behavior and failure to use On Error leads to this behavior. When an error occurs VBA stops on the error line and immediately displays the error message. The application will then require user intervention with the help of a code before it can proceed. It could either mean fixing the error or restarting the application.

According to the example below, On Error line has not been used so VBA will use On Error Goto 0 behavior by default.

Sub UsingDefault()

Dim x **As** Long, y **As Long**

x = 6
y = 6 / 0
x = 7

End Sub

BUG EXTERMINATION TECHNIQUES

A bug is an error in programming; if an application doesn't perform as required then it definitely has a bug. When you begin to write VBA programs, there are high chances the code will have bugs.

Bug extermination is one of the important techniques that a developer should be conversant with.

Programming is about writing code, making mistakes and also fixing them. When you have strong debugging skills, it helps with minimizing the programming cycle and allowing users to pinpoint bugs more quickly. They are also capable of making the necessary fixes that addresses the problems encountered and to verify whether the modifications are correct.

Bugs fall into the following categories;

The logic flaws in your code: Users can avoid these bugs by thinking through the problems that the application addresses carefully.

The incorrect context bugs: These types of bugs come up when you try to execute a task at the wrong time.

The extreme case bugs: These bugs normally come up when

you encounter data that was expected, like very small or large numbers.

The wrong data type bugs: This type occurs whenever you try to process a wrong type of data.

Wrong version bugs: These type of bugs consist of incompatibilities between different versions of Excel.

Beyond your control bugs: These are some of the most frustrating bugs. It may occur when Excel is upgraded and a minor change not documented is made that eventually causes the macros to bomb. Sometimes even security updates can cause problems.

Debugging is the process used to identify and correct bugs that exist within a program and it takes time to develop debugging skills. An understanding between bugs and syntax errors is vital.

A **syntax error** is majorly a language error like misspelling a keyword or omitting a Next statement in a For-Next loop. It may also refer to having a mismatch parenthesis.

A **program bug** on the other hand happens at a more subtle level. You may execute the routine but it may still fail to perform as expected.

. . .

Identification of Bugs

Before any form of debugging can be undertaken, users must determine whether a bug exists. A macro may have a bug if it fails to work as expected. The presence of a bug may be noticed when Excel displays a runtime error message. Bugs tend to appear when least expected and the fact that macros work perfectly with a data set doesn't mean it will work in a similar way with all of the data sets.

One of the best approaches for debugging is by undertaking a thorough testing. You can use a backup copy of your workbook for testing.

DEBUGGING TECHNIQUES

Here are some of the debugging techniques that can be used for Excel VBA code;

Examining the code

One of the basic debugging techniques is to have a closer look at the code then look out for a problem. One should however have some knowledge and experience to effectively use this method.

Use of message box function

One of the common problems with several programs may

involve failure by one or more variables to take on values as required. It's therefore helpful to take time and monitor the variables while the code is running. You can do this by inserting a temporary MsgBox functions into the routine. In case of a variable called CellCount then you can insert this statement;

MsgBox Cellcount

Once you execute the routine, the MsgBox function will display CellCount's value. A message box can be used to display all types of valuable information as the code is running. For example; if a code loops through various sheets then the below statement can display the name and type of the sheet which is active.

MsgBox ActiveSheet .Name & " " & TypeName (ActiveSheet)

If the message box shows something that's not expected then click on Ctrl+Break and a dialog box will emerge with information that "Code execution has been interrupted". You will therefore have the following choices to address the issue;

- Click on continue button and the code will proceed with execution
- Click on the End button and the execution will stop.
- Click on the debug button and the VBE will go into a debug mode.

Inserting Debug. Print statements

This can be used as an alternative to using MsgBox functions within the code. Users can insert temporary Debug.Print statements and the statements can be used to print value of the variables in the next window. The debug.print sends output to the immediate window even if the window is hidden.

Use of Excel built-in debugging tools

Most programmers in Excel are familiar with the bugs concept. Excel program has a set of debugging tools that users can make use of to correct problems that come up in VBA code.

Chapter Nine

EXERCISES: VBA PROGRAMMING EXAMPLES AND TECHNIQUES

BA programming examples and techniques can be organized into the following categories;

- Working with the ranges
- Changing settings in Excel
- Working with charts
- Speeding up the VBA code

Working with the ranges

VBA programming mostly involves worksheet ranges so when working with range objects, the following should be kept in mind. The VBA doesn't have to select a range in order to work with it. If the code selects a range, the actual worksheet should be active. The macro recorder doesn't always generate the most efficient code. You can also create your macro using the recorder then edit the code in order to make it more efficient.

It's advisable to use named ranges in the VBA code. For example use of ("Total") range is far better than ("D45"). If you add any row above row 45 then you should be able to modify the macro so as to use the correct range address as (D46). A range of cells can be named by choosing Formulas>Defined names>Define Name.

When running a macro that works with your current selection range, select entire columns or rows. Excel allows for multiple selections and your code can be used to test for a number of selections before taking appropriate actions.

Copying a range is considered one of the preferred Excel activities. Once you turn the macro recorder on, you can copy a range let's say from A1:A5 to B1:B15 and you will then get this VBA macro;

```
Sub CopyRange()
    Range("A1:A5").Select
    Selection.Copy
    Range("B1").Select
    ActiveSheet.Paste
    Application.CutCopyMode = False
End Sub
```

Copying a variable sized range

In most cases, you may want to copy a given range of cells without having knowledge of the exact column and row dimensions. For example, you may have a workbook that keeps record of weekly sales. It therefore means that the number of rows will keep changing with the addition of new data.

Since you may not be aware of the exact range address; you may need a way of writing code that doesn't use a range address.

	A	B	C	D	E	F
1	Date	Units	Amount			
2	Sep-04	181	6,697			
3	Sep-05	174	5,742			
4	Sep-06	201	7,437			
5	Sep-07	229	8,473			
6	Sep-08	203	6,496			
7	Sep-09	229	7,328			
8	Sep-10	213	8,094			
9	Sep-11	219	8,322			
10	Sep-12	236	7,788			
11	Sep-13	261	8,613			
12	Sep-14	262	8,646			
13						
14						
15						

Sheet1 | Sheet2

The below macro shows how users can copy the range from Sheet 1 to Sheet 2 starting from cell A1.

```
Sub CopyCurrentRegion()
    Range("A1").CurrentRegion.Copy
    Sheets("Sheet2").Select
    Range("A1").Select
    ActiveSheet.Paste
    Sheets("Sheet1").Select
    Application.CutCopyMode = False
End Sub
```

Use of the current region property is similar to choosing Home>Find & Select>GoTo Special> Current region option.

If you are used to combinations such as Ctrl+Shift+Right Arrow and Ctrl+Shift+Down Arrow to select a range consisting of everything including the active cell to end of column or row, then you can write macros that are capable of performing such selections.

VBA can easily accommodate the action and the below procedure can be used to select the range starting with the active cell then extending all the way to the cell right above the first blank cell within the column.

Once you have selected the range, you can move it, copy it, format it or do whatever you desire with it.

```
Sub SelectDown()
    Range(ActiveCell, ActiveCell.End(xlDown)).Select
End Sub
```

Changing Excel Settings

Some of the most important macros are the simple procedures that have the potential of changing Excel procedures. You can begin by changing Boolean settings as they are either on or off.

For example; if you create a macro that turns worksheet page break display on and off; Excel will display dashed lines to indicate page breaks.

The only way to get rid of page break display is by opening Excel options dialog box then click on the advanced tab. You can then scroll down until you locate the show page breaks check box. Once you turn on the macro recorder, Excel will then generate the below code;

ActiveSheet . DisplayPageBreaks = False

If the page breaks are not visible after recording the macro then Excel generates the code below;

ActiveSheet . DisplayPageBreaks = True

To change non-Boolean settings, make use of a select case structure for the non-Boolean settings. The below example shows the calculation mode between the manual and automatic and the displays a message that indicates the current mode:

```
Sub ToggleCalcMode()
    Select Case Application.Calculation
        Case xlManual
            Application.Calculation = xlCalculationAutomatic
            MsgBox "Automatic Calculation Mode"
        Case xlAutomatic
            Application.Calculation = xlCalculationManual
            MsgBox "Manual Calculation Mode"
    End Select
End Sub
```

Working with charts

Charts consist of different objects which makes manipulation of charts with VBA difficult. To modify a chart using VBA you don't have to actually activate the chart, the chart method can instead return the specific chart contained in chart object.

```
Sub ModifyChart1()
    ActiveSheet.ChartObjects("Chart 1").Activate
    ActiveChart.Type = xlArea
End Sub

Sub ModifyChart2()
    ActiveSheet.ChartObjects("Chart 1").Chart.Type = xlArea
End Sub
```

Speeding up the VBA code

VBA is fast although not very fast and there are programming examples that can be used to speed up the macros. When executing Excel macro, you can decide to turn off the screen instead of sitting and watching the execution. You can use the below statement to turn off screen updating;

Application. Screen Updating = False

If you want to see what's happening at anytime within the process of the macro; you can use the below statement to turn back on screen updating.

Application. Screen Updating = True

To express the difference in speed, you can execute this simple macro that fills a range of numbers.

```
Sub FillRange()
    Dim r as Long, c As Long
    Dim Number as Long
    Number = 0
    For r = 1 To 50
        For c = 1 To 50
            Number = Number + 1
            Cells(r, c).Select
            Cells(r, c).Value = Number
        Next c
    Next r
End Sub
```

Communicating with Your Users

The simplest way of communicating with users is through message box and the input box. For a more complex user interaction, it's advisable to use dedicated user forms although it requires some element of work. The message box is used in cases such as;

- When communicating information, an error message or a warning.

- When asking a question

The syntax is: MsgBox (prompt [, buttons] [, title] [, helpfile, context])

Prompt contains string expression that's displayed as a message within the dialog box.

Buttons are optional but contain numeric value that specifies the type and number of buttons to be displayed. The default value of the button is 0.

Title is also optional and contains a string of expression that's displayed in the title bar of the dialog box.

Leveraging Custom Dialog Boxes

It's not possible to be exposed to use Excel for long without being exposed to the dialog boxes which seem to pop up all the time. Excel like other Windows programs makes use of dialog boxes to clarify commands, obtain information and also display messages.

Once you develop Excel macros, you can then create specific dialog boxes that work in a similar way as those built in Excel. The custom dialog boxes are referred to as UserForms in VBA.

Introducing UserForms Basics

Userform is a term used when working in VBA and it refers to dialog boxes. A user form is more like an object which represents a dialog box or a window within Excel user interface.

By working with UserForm object it becomes easier to create custom dialog boxes and each of the created dialog boxes is held within a UserForm object.

Userforms are useful however creating them may take some time. Userforms are useful in cases where the VBA macros have to pause to get information from a user. For example, the macro may have options that can be clearly specified in the userform. If you require more information then you should create userforms.

To create a userform, the following steps should be followed;

- Determine how the dialog box should be used and the point at which it will be displayed in your VBA macro.

- Press Alt+F11 so as to activate the VBE and insert new userForm object.
- Add controls to the userform. The controls consist of items like buttons, text boxes, check boxes and list of boxes.
- Use properties window to modify properties for the controls or the userform itself.
- Write the event handler procedures for controls. The procedures are stored within the code window for the UserForm object.
- Write a procedure which is stored in the VBA module which displays the dialog box.

Creation of a userform is similar to creating Graphical User Interface to the application.

Using UserForm Controls

Once the userform is activated, the VBE then displays toolbox in a floating window. Tools within the toolbox are used for adding controls to the UserForm and if in case the toolbox doesn't appear as you activate the userform, then choose View>Toolbox.

To add control, click on the desired control within the toolbox then drag it into the dialog box so as to create the control. Once you have added control, move and resize it using the standard techniques.

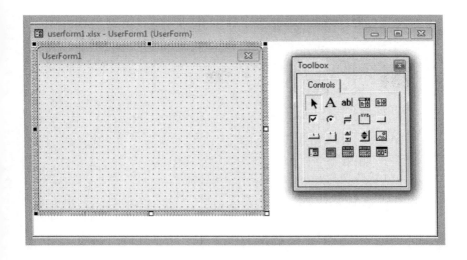

UserForm Toolbox Controls

Control

What it does

Label

Shows text

TextBox

Allows the user to enter text

Combo Box

Displays a drop-down list

ListBox

Displays a list of items

CheckBox

Useful for yes/no or off/on options

Option Button

Used in groups and allows users to select the options

Toggle Button

A button that is either on or off

Frame
Container for other controls
Command Button
A clickable button
Tab strip
Displays tab
Multipage
A tabbed container for other objects
Scrollbar
A draggable bar
SpinButton
A clickable button often used for changing a given value
Image
Holds an image
RefEdit
Allows users to select a range.

UserForm Techniques and Tricks

The ability to create userforms or custom dialog boxes is very useful. Before you create userform, it's important to take time and check if everything is in place.

You can look out for the following;

1. Whether the controls are aligned with each other
2. Do controls that are similar have the same size?
3. Are the controls evenly spaced
4. Is the dialog box overwhelming?
5. Is it possible to access the control using an accelerator key?

6. Are any of the accelerator keys duplicated?
7. Is the tab order correctly set? The user should be able to navigate through the dialog box easily and also access the controls well.
8. Will the VBA code take appropriate action in case the userform is canceled or if the user presses on escape?
9. If the userform will be used in different versions, have you taken time to test in different versions?

Once you have added controls to your userform, the next step is to develop a VBA code that can be displayed in the dialog box. You can do that by selecting Insert>module to insert a VBAmodule.

The next step is to enter the below macro;

Sub GetData ()
UserForm1 .Show
End Sub

To make the macro available, activate Excel then choose Developer>Controls>Insert then click the button icon in the Form Controls area. Drag it into the worksheet in order to create the button.

The assign macro dialog box then appears and you can assign the GetData macro to the button and edit the button's caption for it to read Data Entry.

UserForm Examples

To create a userform follow the steps below

- Insert a UserForm
- Add controls to the Userform
- Resize or move the added Userform controls as desired.
- Custom the Userform or controls
- Assign a VBA code to the UserForm
- Load or display the UserForm
- Hide or close the UserForm.

To add controls to your Userform, you should follow the below steps

- Begin by opening the visual basic editor. If in case the project explorer is not visible; you should click on view project explorer.

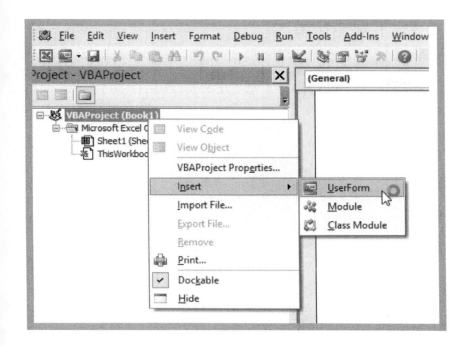

- Click on insert userform and if the toolbox doesn't automatically appear, click on view then toolbox. Your screen will then show as below;

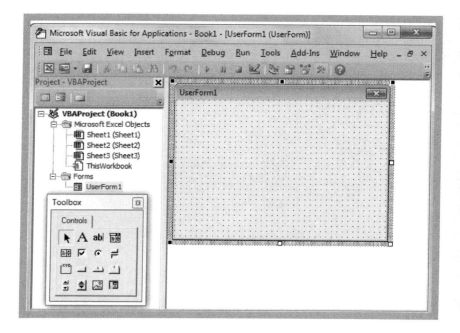

- The next step is to add the controls as shown in the earlier list and the result should be consistent with the UserForm picture.

- You can change names and captions of controls as a good practice so as to make the code much easier to read. Click on view then properties window to change the names and captions then click on each control.

In order to show the userform; place a command button on your worksheet then add the below code.

```
Private Sub CommandButton1_Click()
DinnerPlannerUserForm.Show
End Sub
```

Accessing Your Macros through the User Interface

The ribbon is Microsoft Office user interface and it can be modified or customized by using VBA. If you write an application and want to add more buttons to the ribbon, program the changes outside of Excel by using RibbonX.

Making changes manually to the ribbon is normally easy however one should use Excel 2010 or 2013. Here are the steps that can be used to customize the ribbon;

Tabs

- Add a custom tab
- Delete custom tab
- Add a new group to tab
- Change the order of tabs

- Change a tab's name
- Hide built-in tabs

Groups

- Add new custom groups
- Add commands to a custom group
- Remove groups from a tab
- Move group to a different tab
- Change the groups order within a tab
- Change a group name

As you customize the ribbon there are some tasks you cannot do regardless of how hard you try. It's impossible to remove the built-in tabs however you can hide them. You cannot remove the commands from the built-in groups. You also can'tchange the commands order within a built-in group.

Manual changes to the ribbon can be made by customizing the ribbon panel of Excel Options dialog box. You can do that by right clicking anywhere within the ribbon then choosing customize the ribbon.

To add a macro to the ribbon, customize the ribbon to also include a macro. The macro command is visible in the ribbon and once you click on the command a workbook that contains the macro will open. If you add a button that executes macro to the ribbon, the ribbon modification will apply to your Excel copy. Modifications to the ribbon are not part of the workbook and may not appear if you share the workbook with another person.

There are instances where you may automatically modify the ribbon especially when add-ins or a workbook is opened. It therefore becomes easier for the macro to be accessed by the user. It also eliminates any need by the user to modify the ribbon manually through use of Excel options dialog box.

Making changes to the ribbon automatically can be done with Excel 2007 and other later versions although it isn't a simple task. Modifying the ribbon entails writing of XML code in the text editor then copying the XML file over to the workbook file. It entails editing several XML files which is generally a zipped collection of files and then writing VBA procedures to handle clicking of controls that are put in the XML file.

You can follow the steps below;

- Create a new Excel workbook
- Save the workbook then name it ribbon modification.xlsm
- Close the workbook.

- Launch custom UI editor for Microsoft Office (Get the software if you don't have it)
- In the custom UI editor choose File>Open then find the saved workbook.
- Choose Insert>Office 2007 Custom UI Part (Choose this command even if you are using a higher version of Excel)
- Type the below code into the code panel

```xml
<customUI xmlns='http://schemas.microsoft.com/
         office/2006/01/customui'>
<ribbon>
<tabs>
<tab idMso='TabHome'>
  <group id='Group1' label='Excel VBA For Dummies'>
    <button id='Button1'
        label='Click Me'
        size='large'
        onAction='ShowMessage'
        imageMso='FileStartWorkflow' />
  </group>
</tab>
</tabs>
</ribbon>
</customUI>
```

- Click on the validate button in the toolbar. If the code has syntax errors then you will get a message that describes the specific problem. Ensure that you correct the errors once identified.
- Return to the custom UI.xml module then choose File>Save.
- Close the file using File>Close command

- Open the workbook in Excel by clicking on the Home tab.
- Press on Alt+F11 to activate the VBE.
- Insert a new VBA module then paste the callback procedure that was generated earlier. Add a MsgBox statement so that you can know if the procedure is being executed.
- Press Alt+F11 to get to Excel then click on a new button over the ribbon. If well executed, you will see the message as below.

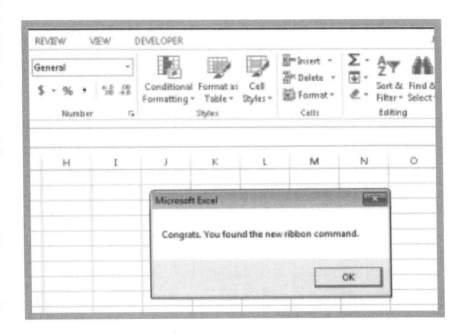

Putting it all Together

For those who are great at creating macros and programming, the ability to create custom worksheet functions is one thing that attracts many to VBA. Custom functions provide users with an added working advantage as they are able to work as they desire.

∼

CREATING WORKSHEET FUNCTIONS

A majority of Excel users are familiar with Excel worksheet functions such as IF, AVERAGE and SUM. Excel has over 450 worksheet functions and users are free to create more functions through use of VBA.

Functions are still required in order to make the work simpler and with some element of planning, worksheet formulas and VBA procedures are quite useful for simplifying work.

A VBA function refers to a procedure stored within a VBA module. The functions can also be used in other VBA procedures or within the worksheet formulas.

Custom functions cannot be created using a macro recorder even though a macro recorder may help with identifying the relevant properties and methods.

A module may contain a number of functions and if the function is defined within a different workbook then it should be preceded with a function name and the workbook name. A function name acts more like a variable with the final value of the variable being that returned by the function.

Here is an example of a function that returns the first name of the user;

```
Function FirstName()
    Dim FullName As String
    Dim FirstSpace As Integer
    FullName = Application.UserName
    FirstSpace = InStr(FullName, " ")
    If FirstSpace = 0 Then
        FirstName = FullName
    Else
        FirstName = Left(FullName, FirstSpace - 1)
    End If
End Function
```

Creating Excel Add-Ins

The capability to create add-ins is another great feature in Excel. An Excel ad-in is a feature that is added to help with enhancing the functionality of Excel. Some of the add-ins provide users with new worksheet functions that can be used in formulas. Other add-ins also provide a set of new commands or utilities. A properly designed add-in will have its new features blend well with that of the original interface so as to become part of the program.

Excel comes with a variety of add-ins alongside solver and analysis Toolpak. There are also add-ins from third party suppliers. Any user who is knowledgeable is capable of creating add-ins however VBA programming skills are vital.

Reasons for creating Add-Ins

Makes it more difficult to access your code

- Helps with eliminating confusion
- Simplifies access to the worksheet functions.
- Provides easy access for users
- Allows better access for users
- Helps in avoiding display of prompts when unloading

You can load and unload the add-ins by using add-ins dialog box. To display the dialog box go to file>options>add-ins and then select Excel add-ins from the drop-down list at the bottom of the dialog screen then click on go.

Creating an add-in is never difficult however it requires some extra work. You can follow the below steps to create an add-in.

1. Develop the application and ensure that everything is working properly. Remember to also include a method for executing the macros.
2. You can test the application by executing it when using another active workbook
3. Activate VBE then select workbook within the project window. Choose tools >VBA project properties then click on the protection tab and select

the lock project for viewing check box then enter a password twice and click on OK.
4. Select Developer>Document Panel then click on Ok to for the standard properties panel to be displayed.
5. In the document properties panel, add a brief title in the title field and some description in the comment field.
6. Choose File>Save As then select add-in (*.xlam) from the save as type drop down list.
7. Specify the folder for storing the add-in then click on save. A copy of the workbook will then be converted to an add-in and will be saved with XLAM extension. The original workbook however remains open.

Chapter Ten

ADVANCED VBA TECHNIQUES

Working with Pivot Tables

Pivot tables are similar in function to data mining and extraction in spreadsheets. A pivot table is created by using a named range then only filtering the data you intend to use in your reports.

Pivot table can be created using VBA or in the IDE and both of the methods work well with Excel.

Before you create a pivot table in VBA you should have a basic understanding on how Pivot Table works. VBA makes it possible to create a dynamic pivot table through use of code. Before you start creating the pivot table with VBA, ensure that you open the Visual Basic Editor then create a module right from the project manager.

. . .

Here are the steps to follow when creating pivot table in VBA;

Declare Variables

The first step is to declare the variables which should be used in the code to define different things.

```
'Declare Variables
Dim PSheet As Worksheet
Dim DSheet As Worksheet
Dim PCache As PivotCache
Dim PTable As PivotTable
Dim PRange As Range
Dim LastRow As Long
Dim LastCol As Long
```

The above code declares that;

PSheet: To create a sheet for the new pivot table

DSheet: To be used as data sheet

PChache: To be used as a name for the pivot table cache

PTable: To be used as a name for the pivot table

PRange: To be used in defining source data range

LastRow and LastCol: To be used to get the last row and column of the data range.

Insert a new worksheet

Before creating the pivot table, Excel inserts a blank sheet and then creates a new pivot table. Once a new worksheet has been created, the code below will be used in setting the value of PSheet variable and DSheet to pivot table worksheet and data worksheet.

```
'Insert a New Blank Worksheet
On Error Resume Next
Application.DisplayAlerts = False
Worksheets("PivotTable").Delete
Sheets.Add Before:=ActiveSheet
ActiveSheet.Name = "PivotTable"
Application.DisplayAlerts = True
Set PSheet = Worksheets("PivotTable")
Set DSheet = Worksheets("Data")
```

If you want to change the name of the worksheet, do that from the code. You will need a code capable of identifying the entire data from the source sheet. Here is the code;

```
'Define Data Range
LastRow = DSheet.Cells(Rows.Count, 1).End(xlUp).Row
LastCol = DSheet.Cells(1, Columns.Count).End(xlToLeft).Column
Set PRange = DSheet.Cells(1, 1).Resize(LastRow, LastCol)
```

Create a pivot cache

Before you create a pivot table, you need to create a pivot cache and define the data source. Here is the code for pivot cache;

```
'Define Pivot Cache
Set PCache = ActiveWorkbook.PivotCaches.Create _
(SourceType:=xlDatabase, SourceData:=PRange). _
CreatePivotTable(TableDestination:=PSheet.Cells(2, 2), _
TableName:="SalesPivotTable")
```

Insert a blank pivot table

When creating a pivot table, you will get a blank pivot first then you can define the values, columns and rows. Use the code below to insert a pivot table;

```
'Insert Blank Pivot Table
Set PTable = PCache.CreatePivotTable _
(TableDestination:=PSheet.Cells(1, 1),
TableName:="SalesPivotTable")
```

Insert the row and column fields

Once you have created a blank pivot table, you can insert the row and column fields as normal. You should however write a code for each of the rows and column. The column below shows addition of years and month in the row field and zones into the column field.

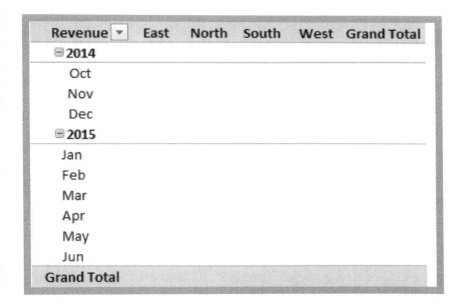

Here is the code to use;

```
'Insert Row Fields
With
ActiveSheet.PivotTables("SalesPivotTable").PivotFields("Year")
.Orientation = xlRowField
.Position = 1
End With

With
ActiveSheet.PivotTables("SalesPivotTable").PivotFields("Month")
.Orientation = xlRowField
.Position = 2
End With
```

```
'Insert Column Fields
With
ActiveSheet.PivotTables("SalesPivotTable").PivotFields("Zone")
.Orientation = xlColumnField
.Position = 1
End With
```

Insert data field

The next step is to define the value fields within the pivot table. The code below can be used to add the value fields;

```
'Insert Data Field

With ActiveSheet.PivotTables("SalesPivotTable").PivotFields("Amount")

.Orientation = xlDataField

.Position = 1

.Function = xlSum

.NumberFormat = "#,##0"

.Name = "Revenue "

End With
```

The above code formats value as a number that has (,) separator.

Format Pivot Table

You will need to use a code to format the pivot table. The formatting style can be defined within the code when using VBA.

Revenue	Column Labels				
Row Labels	East	North	South	West	Grand Total
⊟ 2014	1,503,051	5,206,566	3,793,021	19,189	10,521,827
Oct	220,784	874,476	589,860		1,685,120
Nov	527,246	2,122,459	1,493,348		4,143,053
Dec	755,021	2,209,631	1,709,813	19,189	4,693,654
⊟ 2015	6,692,173	17,508,578	11,802,135	4,338,775	40,341,661
Jan	1,074,617	2,749,852	1,687,593	398,206	5,910,268
Feb	800,108	2,834,240	1,586,336	486,828	5,707,512
Mar	993,920	3,102,326	1,984,760	799,455	6,880,461
Apr	898,759	3,168,095	2,185,258	993,599	7,245,711
May	1,407,726	3,043,954	2,250,576	896,530	7,598,786
Jun	1,517,043	2,610,111	2,107,612	764,157	6,998,923
Grand Total	8,195,224	22,715,144	15,595,156	4,357,964	50,863,488

The code to be used for the pivot table is;

```
'Format Pivot Table
ActiveSheet.PivotTables("SalesPivotTable").ShowTableStyleRowStripes = True
ActiveSheet.PivotTables("SalesPivotTable").TableStyle2 = "PivotStyleMedium9"
```

Working with Charts

Since a lot of time is spent in creating graphs and charts, having knowledge of how to automate them can be helpful. You can easily manipulate charts and graphs with the help of VBA code.

To insert a chart, here is one of the methods you can use.

```
Sub CreateChart()
'PURPOSE: Create a chart (chart dimensions are not required)

Dim rng As Range
Dim cht As Object

'Your data range for the chart
  Set rng = ActiveSheet.Range("A24:M27")

'Create a chart
  Set cht = ActiveSheet.Shapes.AddChart2

'Give chart some data
  cht.Chart.SetSourceData Source:=rng

'Determine the chart type
  cht.Chart.ChartType = xlXYScatterLines

End Sub
```

To loop through charts use the below code;

```vba
Sub LoopThroughCharts()
'PURPOSE: How to cycle through charts and chart series

Dim cht As ChartObject
Dim ser As Series

'Loop Through all charts on ActiveSheet
  For Each cht In ActiveSheet.ChartObjects

  Next cht

'Loop through all series in a chart
  For Each ser In grph.Chart.SeriesCollection

  Next ser

'Loop Through all series on Activesheet
  For Each cht In ActiveSheet.ChartObjects
    For Each ser In grph.Chart.SeriesCollection

    Next ser
  Next cht

End Sub
```

To add and also modify a chart title use the code below;

```vba
Sub AddChartTitle()
'PURPOSE: Add a title to a specific chart

Dim cht As ChartObject

Set cht = ActiveSheet.ChartObjects("Chart 1")

'Ensure chart has a title
  cht.Chart.HasTitle = True

'Change chart's title
  cht.Chart.ChartTitle.Text = "My Graph"

End Sub
```

Interacting with Other applications

Users can interact with other applications by using VBA. You can interact with applications such as PowerPoint, Word, Outlook and others. You can also interact with other applications like SAS, Explorer, etc.

In order to do that, you should first establish a connection with the applications then you will be able to access objects of those applications from the VBA. Connection can be established either through early or late binding. In case you want to automate other Microsoft applications, you will have to declare variables over your procedure. You should be able to declare the object variables that are specific to the application you intend to automate.

If you want to interact with Ms Word then you have to write the code as below;

```
Dim wordApp As Word.Application
Dim wordDoc As Word.Document

' Reference existing instance of Word
    Set wordApp = GetObject(, &amp;quot;Word.Application&amp;quot;)
' Reference active document
    Set wordDoc = wordApp.ActiveDocument
```

CONCLUSION

Congratulations and thank you for investing in this book and reading it through to the end. Excel is such a powerful program that many people fail to maximize its capability due to lack of sufficient knowledge on how they can make use of it.

Use of Excel VBA is not a preserve for only those well versed with programming but beginners can equally learn and master VBA for enhanced use of Excel program. Instead of spending huge amounts of time in doing repetitive tasks, you can make the most of your time as you begin to implement the knowledge you have acquired on Excel VBA.

Most of the information acquired from this book is actionable and requires only some level of practice to gain deep insight into what VBA is about and how to make use of it for enhanced performance within Excel.

Now that you have acquired some vital information about Excel, I encourage you to take your time and implement that which you have learnt.

I do have a request; would you kindly go ahead and leave a review for this book.

Thank you and enjoy implementing Excel VBA.

REFERENCES

https://powerspreadsheets.com

https://www.thespreadsheetguru.com

https://blog.programminghub.io

https://excelchamps.com

Printed in Poland
by Amazon Fulfillment
Poland Sp. z o.o., Wrocław